W9-CLJ-595

Of Numbers and Stars

The Story of Hypatia

BY D. ANNE LOVE

ILLUSTRATED BY PAM PAPARONE

Holiday House / New York

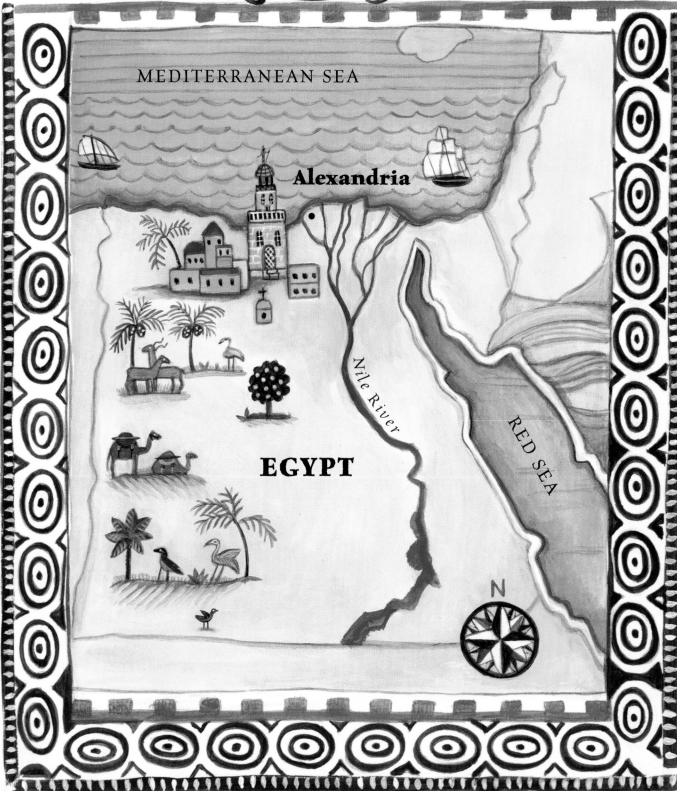

MEDITERRANEAN SEA

Alexandria

Nile River

EGYPT

RED SEA

N

ON THE NORTHERN TIP OF EGYPT, where the Nile River meets the Mediterranean Sea, stands the ancient city of Alexandria. Established by Alexander the Great more than two thousand years ago, the city soon became a center of learning and trade. Scholars from all over the world came to study at the university and to read the scrolls in the great library. Glassblowing, linen weaving, and papermaking flourished. Spices and perfumes, barley and dates went by ship and caravan to faraway places.

By the fourth century C E, Alexandria was home to several hundred thousand people who lived in graceful houses set along wide streets.

It was a city of theaters and lecture halls, taverns and workshops. Artists made murals and mosaics to decorate the buildings where laws were made. In houses and on busy street corners, philosophers, astronomers, and mathematicians gathered to debate the important ideas of the day.

One day in the house of Theon, a baby girl was born. From the very beginning she was a beautiful child, round and rosy. Her parents named her Hypatia. Had she been born into an ordinary household, perhaps we might never have heard of her again, for girls who lived in Alexandria so long ago had few rights. Hardly any of them learned to read or write. Many became servants.

Perhaps Hypatia's mother planned to teach her how to manage a fine house, how to weave and cook and sew. But her father had other ideas.

"A girl should be educated in the same way as a boy," Theon declared. "I will teach her everything I know."

Since he was a professor at the university, he knew many things. As soon as Hypatia learned to walk, he set about keeping his promise.

Under her father's watchful eyes,
Hypatia learned to swim in the calm, sun-bright sea.
She learned the names of all the fishes
and how to catch them with a spear.

She learned to ride a horse, pressing her knees to its sleek sides. To the astonishment of most other girls, who could only watch from their windows, up and down the street Hypatia rode, past the linen weaver's shop, past the glassblowers and the silk merchants and papyrus makers, past the shop where her mother bought perfumed oils for the family's lamps.

One summer Hypatia learned
to row a boat, practicing until she could
steer it through the sea as straight
and silent as an arrow. Her father was pleased
with all she had mastered, but there was
much more to learn.

Every day, Hypatia practiced
reading and writing.
She learned grammar and
the proper way of speaking.
She read the works
of great poets.

She studied science, learning the names of the reeds and trees
and sweet-smelling blossoms that grew near her house.

She studied the ways of the birds and
the night creatures, and learned to
name the pictures the stars painted
in the dark, windy sky.

One day Hypatia rode her horse to the university to visit her father. Leaning over his shoulder, she watched him write sentences made not of words, but of numbers. She saw the patterns the numbers made. To her they were more beautiful than the patterns on her mother's favorite urn. One look at his daughter's expectant face told Theon all he needed to know.

"We shall begin with arithmetic," he said. "Later you will learn geometry and astronomy."

And so they began. In time, Hypatia knew all about numbers
and lines, triangles and squares.

She learned to track the movements of Mercury and Venus, Mars and Jupiter and Saturn across the night sky and to predict the time of the rising and setting of the sun.

CONFUCIUS
551-479 BC

ARISTOTLE
384-322 BC

PLATO
427-347 BC

Hypatia also studied philosophy—which meant she spent a lot of time thinking about *thinking*. In search of true wisdom, she read the pronouncements of the oracles, and debated with her father questions of values and the science of reasoning.

MARCUS AURELIUS
ANTONIUS
AD 121-180

BUDDHA
563-483 BC

SOCRATES
469-399 BC

Soon Hypatia became a young woman noted for her wisdom and scholarship. Dressed in a *tribon*, the robe of a scholar, she lectured in public places around the city and at her home, where a constant stream of students from wealthy and important families absorbed her every word. Some came from Alexandria or other towns in Egypt. Others arrived from Syria, Cyrene, and Constantinople. Most studied with the woman they called "beloved teacher" for many years, then went on to important jobs in the church or in the government.

With her father, Hypatia wrote books to explain the work of other scholars. Quiet and dignified, she won the respect of the city's leaders, many of whom came to call on her as soon as they were installed in office.

After a time, Hypatia's fame spread to other parts of the world. She received letters from other scholars eager for her opinions on math or science or philosophy. Following Hypatia's advice, her devoted student Synesius developed an instrument called an astrolabe. The astrolabe helped sailors measure the angle between the sun and the horizon. It helped them determine latitude and find true north as they journeyed across the sea.

Although there were other women philosophers living at this time, none became as famous or beloved as Hypatia. Through her extraordinary roles as scholar, philosopher, writer, and teacher, she became a symbol of learned women for centuries to come.

Author's Note

Hypatia (High-PAY-shah) was to pay a price for her fame. Although scholars continue to debate whether she was killed for her refusal to embrace Christianity or for political reasons, there is a general agreement on the details of her death.

Cyril, who became patriarch of Alexandria around the year 412, perhaps fearing Hypatia's continuing popularity, urged a group of fanatics to attack her as she was driving in her chariot. They dragged her into the street, pulled out her hair, then killed her. Despite demands from her friends for an investigation into her death, no one was ever charged with the crime.

For more than fifteen hundred years, Hypatia's contributions to mathematics and philosophy were lost or ignored, but modern scholars are once again recognizing her role in the development of these disciplines.

More About Math

The word *mathematics* comes from a Greek word meaning "inclined to learn."

In prehistoric times, people used pebbles or made marks on pieces of wood or bone to record the size of animal herds or the number of fish taken from the sea.

The ancient Egyptians invented the decimal system almost five thousand years ago. They were also the first to use geometry. They needed geometry to figure out how to build the pyramids and how to measure their fields after the Nile River flooded.

The Babylonians invented the sexagesimal system, which is based on groups of sixty.

We still use this system today to measure time in hours, minutes, and seconds.

Until the tenth century CE, the Romans used letters to represent numbers. In Roman numerals, I=1, V=5, X=10, L=50, C=100, D=500, and M=1,000. Other numbers were made by adding to or subtracting from these values. A bar over a number was used to show multiplication by 1,000.

Bibliography

Because Hypatia lived so many years ago, there is very little firsthand information available about her life and work. Parts of letters from her student Synesius survive, as do descriptions of her fame as a teacher from such writers as Socrates Scholasticus and Damascius. Scholars today, using their own interpretations of existing records and relying on their own suppositions, differ on many aspects of her life and work. Here are some of the sources I used in writing this book:

Bowersock, G. W., Peter Brown, and Oleg Grabar, eds. *Late Antiquity: A Guide to the Postclassical World.* Cambridge, Mass.: Belknap Press of Harvard University Press, 1999.

Dzielska, Maria. *Hypatia of Alexandria.* Cambridge, Mass.: Harvard University Press, 1995.

Empereur, Jean-Yves. *Alexandria Rediscovered.* New York: George Braziller, 1996.

I am indebted to Professor M. A. B. Deakin, Department of Mathematics, Monash University, Clayton, Victoria, Australia, who generously shared with me the results of his own scholarship regarding Hypatia and her work.

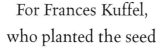

For Frances Kuffel,
who planted the seed
D. A. L.

For Andrea
P. P.

Text copyright © 2006 by D. Anne Love
Illustrations copyright © 2006 by Pam Paparone
All Rights Reserved
Printed in the United States of America
The artwork was created with acrylics.
The text typeface is Celestia Antiqua.
www.holidayhouse.com
First Edition
1 3 5 7 9 10 8 6 4 2

Library of Congress Cataloging-in-Publication Data
Love, D. Anne.
Of numbers and stars: the story of Hypatia /
by D. Anne Love ; illustrated by Pam Paparone.—1st ed.
p. cm.
Includes bibliographical references.
ISBN 0-8234-1621-6
1. Hypatia, d. 415—Juvenile literature.
2. Mathematicians—Egypt—Biography—
Juvenile literature. 3. Women mathematicians—
Egypt—Biography—Juvenile literature.
4. Philosophers—Egypt—Biography—
Juvenile literature. 5. Women philosophers—Egypt—
Biography—Juvenile literature.
[1. Hypatia, d. 415. 2. Mathematicians.
3. Philosophers.
4. Women—Biography.]
I. Paparone, Pam, ill. II. Title.
QA29.H88L68 2005
510'.92—dc22
2003064725
ISBN-13: 978-0-8234-1621-9
ISBN-10: 0-8234-1621-6